STAR WARS™

WORKBOOKS

MATHS SKILLS

FOR AGES 7–8

BY THE EDITORS OF BRAIN QUEST

EDUCATIONAL CONSULTANT: CHARLOTTE RABY

SCHOLASTIC

Scholastic Children's Books
Euston House,
24 Eversholt Street,
London NW1 1DB, UK

A division of Scholastic Ltd
London ~ New York ~ Toronto ~ Sydney ~ Auckland
Mexico City ~ New Delhi ~ Hong Kong

First published in the USA by Workman Publishing in 2014.
This edition published in the UK by Scholastic Ltd in 2016.
© & TM 2016 LUCASFILM LTD.

STAR WARS is a registered trademark of Lucasfilm Ltd.
BRAIN QUEST is a registered trademark of Workman Publishing Co., Inc., and Groupe Play Bac, S.A.

Workbook series design by Raquel Jaramillo
Cover illustration by Mike Sutfin
Interior illustrations by Lawrence Christmas

ISBN 978 1407 16294 2

Printed in Malaysia

4 6 8 10 9 7 5

www.scholastic.co.uk

STAR WARS™
WORKBOOKS

This workbook belongs to:

_____

Revise Place Value

You can use **place value** to work out how much numerals are worth. Look at **32**:

tens   ones

The **3** tells us there are **3 tens**.
The **2** tells us there are **2 ones**.

Look at the numerals and words below each card.

Write the number they equal on the line.

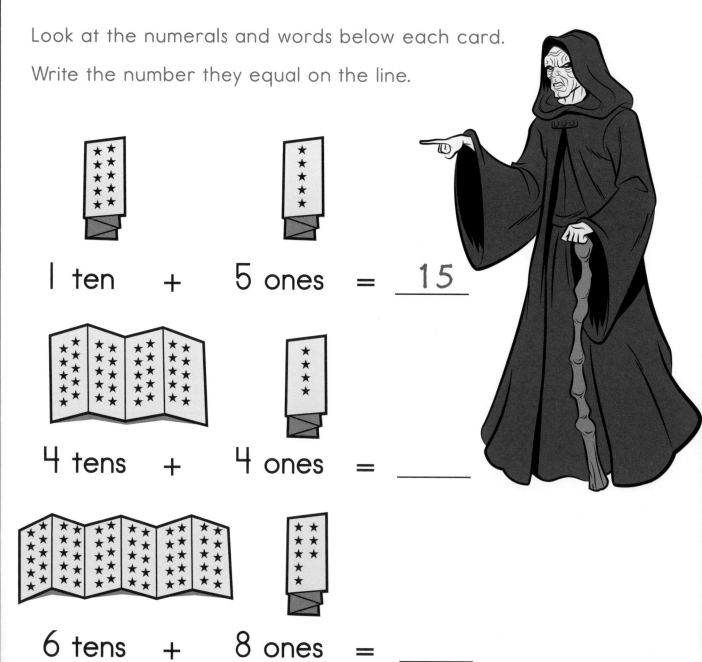

1 ten   +   5 ones   =   15

4 tens   +   4 ones   =   ____

6 tens   +   8 ones   =   ____

9 tens   +   0 ones   =   ____

3 tens   +   7 ones   =   ____

5 tens   +   1 one   =   ____

2 tens   +   6 ones   =   ____

7 tens   +   9 ones   =   ____

Hundreds

If you see three numerals, you know that the number is made up of **hundreds**, **tens** and **ones**. Look at **642**:

6̸4̸2̸

↗ ↗ ↗
hundreds tens ones

The **6** tells us there are **6 hundreds**.
The **4** tells us there are **4 tens**.
The **2** tells us there are **2 ones**.

Circle the correct numeral.

Circle the **ones**.   56③

Circle the **tens**.   84

Circle the **hundreds**.   125

Circle the **tens**.   368

Circle the **hundreds**.   620

Circle the **ones**.   56

Circle the **hundreds**.   157

Circle the **ones**.   917

Circles the **tens**.   586

Look at each number.

Then answer the questions.

275   How many hundreds? __2__   tens? __7__   ones? __5__

481   How many hundreds? _____   tens? _____   ones? _____

802   How many hundreds? _____   tens? _____   ones? _____

689   How many hundreds? _____   tens? _____   ones? _____

743   How many hundreds? _____   tens? _____   ones? _____

500   How many hundreds? _____   tens? _____   ones? _____

318   How many hundreds? _____   tens? _____   ones? _____

957   How many hundreds? _____   tens? _____   ones? _____

45   How many hundreds? _____   tens? _____   ones? _____

113   How many hundreds? _____   tens? _____   ones? _____

More Hundreds

Write the **place value** for each numeral on the chart.

	hundreds	tens	ones
426	4	2	6
193			
501			
978			
345			
109			
272			
486			
814			
768			
659			
321			

Draw a line to match the words to the number.

6 hundreds, 1 ten, 7 ones

3 hundreds, 2 tens, 8 ones

4 hundreds, 9 tens

2 hundreds, 5 tens, 2 ones

9 hundreds, 1 one

8 hundreds, 3 tens, 4 ones

7 ones

1 hundred, 7 tens, 3 ones

834

173

328

490

7

617

252

901

Words to Numbers

Draw a line to match the words to the number.

5 hundreds, 1 ten   32

8 tens, 8 ones   285

3 tens, 2 ones   943

1 hundred, 2 tens, 3 ones   701

7 hundreds, 1 one   510

2 hundreds, 8 tens, 5 ones   123

9 hundreds, 4 tens, 3 ones   88

Write out the number **529** using words:

_____

_____

Write the numbers on the sandcrawlers.

forty-seven

twenty-two

one hundred and thirty-eight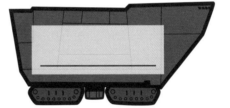

three hundred and twelve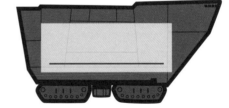

seven hundred and eighty-nine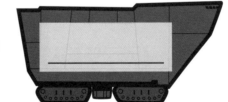

six hundred and eighteen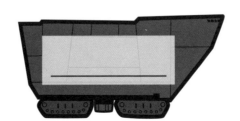

nine hundred and two

My Numbers

Write how many of each you have in the chart.

Then answer the questions.

Parents	Siblings	Pets	Grand-parents	Aunts	Uncles	Wookiees

Which do you have the most of? _____

Least? _____

Are any the same number? _____

Complete the sentences with numbers.

Then write the numbers in words on the line.

I am _____ years old.

_____

I am _____ centimetres tall.

_____

I have _____ lightsabers.

_____

You're Invited!

The Ewoks are having a party for your birthday! Help them write the invitation by filling in the blanks.

Write the numbers in words.

_____
your name

will be _____ years old on
             age

_____   _____
        day   month

Where: _____
              house number and street

_____ , _____
     town or city   county

When: _____
                      date

At: _____
                    time

Revise > or <

Write the number of candles beneath each birthday cake.
Then write **>** or **<** to show which cake has more candles.

< means **less than**.

> means **greater than**.

_11_   _<_   _14_

___   ___   ___

___   ___   ___

___   ___   ___

More or Less?

Write **>** or **<** to show which group has more clone troopers.

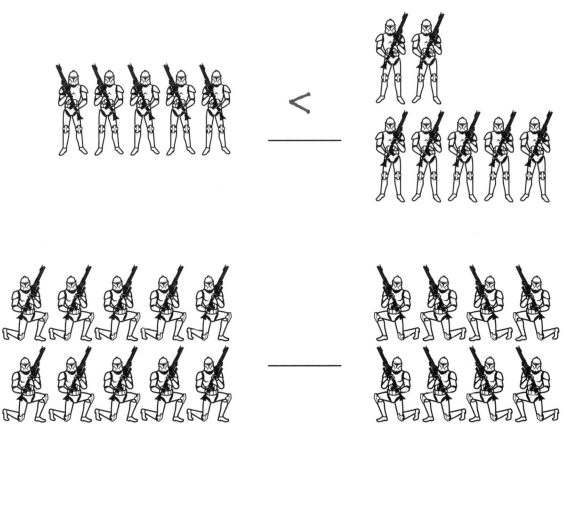

 —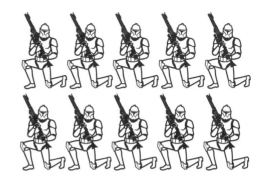

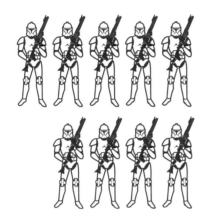 —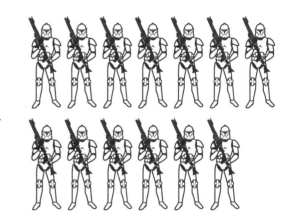

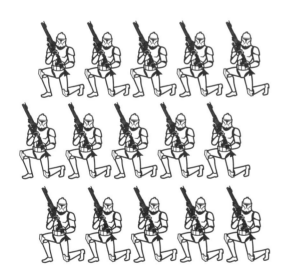 —

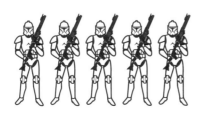 —

Comparing Lightsabers

Compare the number of lightsabers.

Write > or < to show which group has more lightsabers.

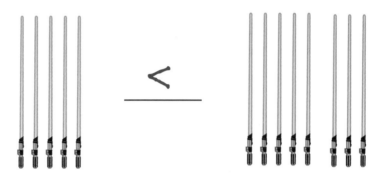

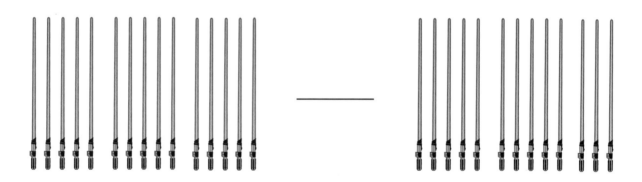

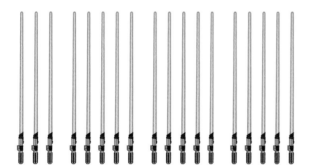
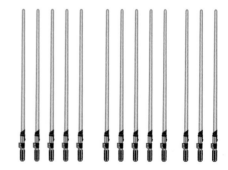

Write > or < to show which number is greater.

12 _<_ 17

364 ____ 346

98 ____ 100

289 ____ 198

45 ____ 65

500 ____ 600

11 ____ 21

823 ____ 843

88 ____ 8

900 ____ 899

102 ____ 103

240 ____ 340

Count in Threes!

Fill in the missing numbers in the smoke trail.

_3_ _6_ _9_ ___ ___ ___ _21_ ___ ___ ___ ___ ___ ___ ___

Count in Fours!

Fill in the missing numbers on the shipping containers.

Count in Fives!

Fill in the missing numbers in the bubbles.

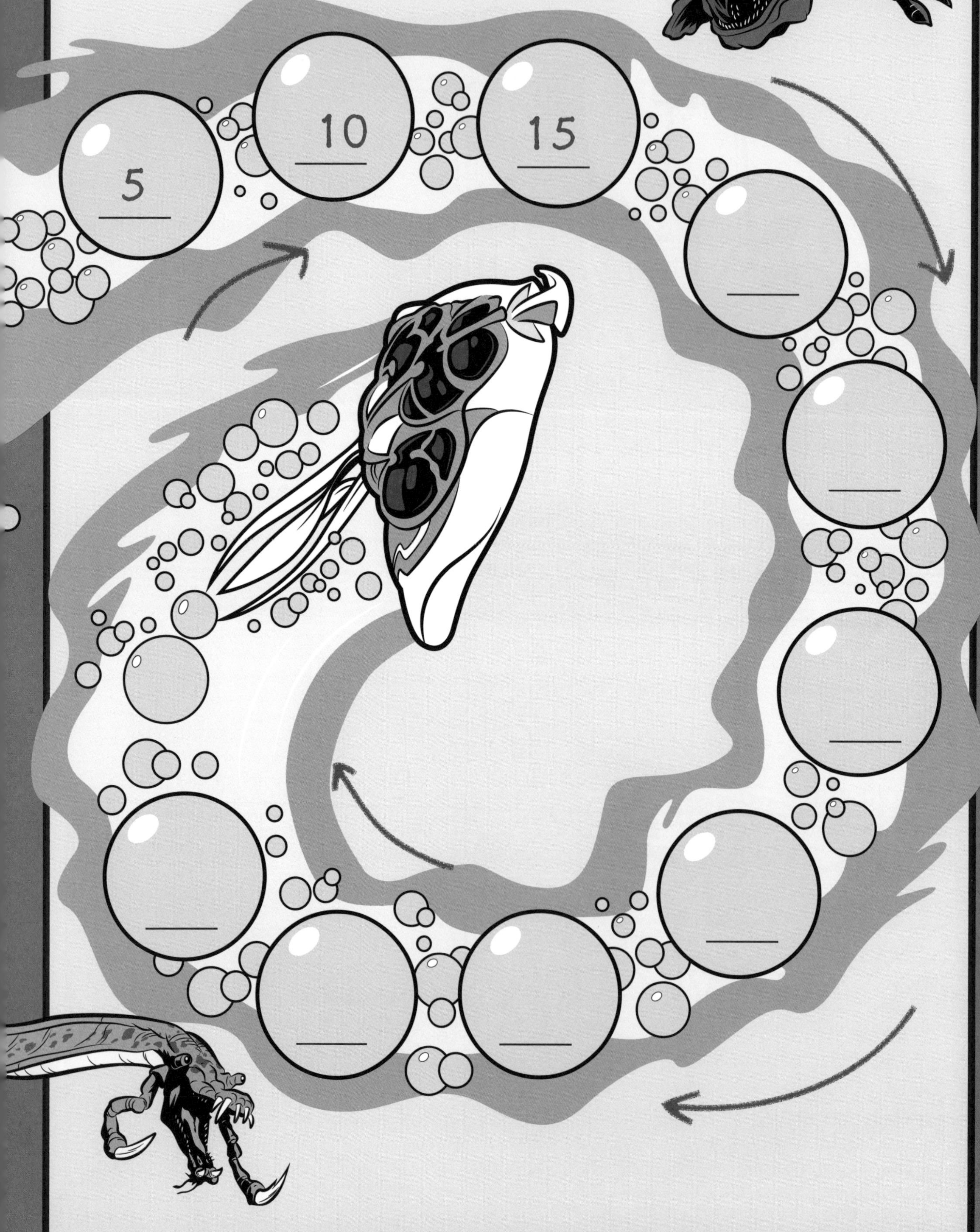

5

10

15

___

___

___

___

___

___

___

Count in Eights!

Fill in the missing numbers on the flags.

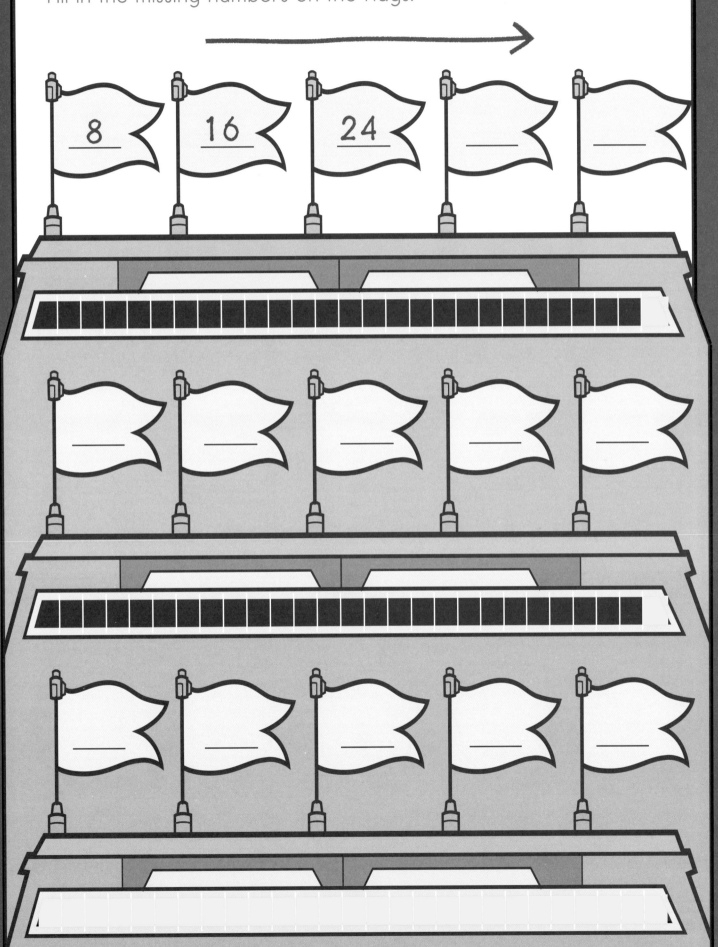

Count in Fifties!

Fill in the missing numbers on the droids.

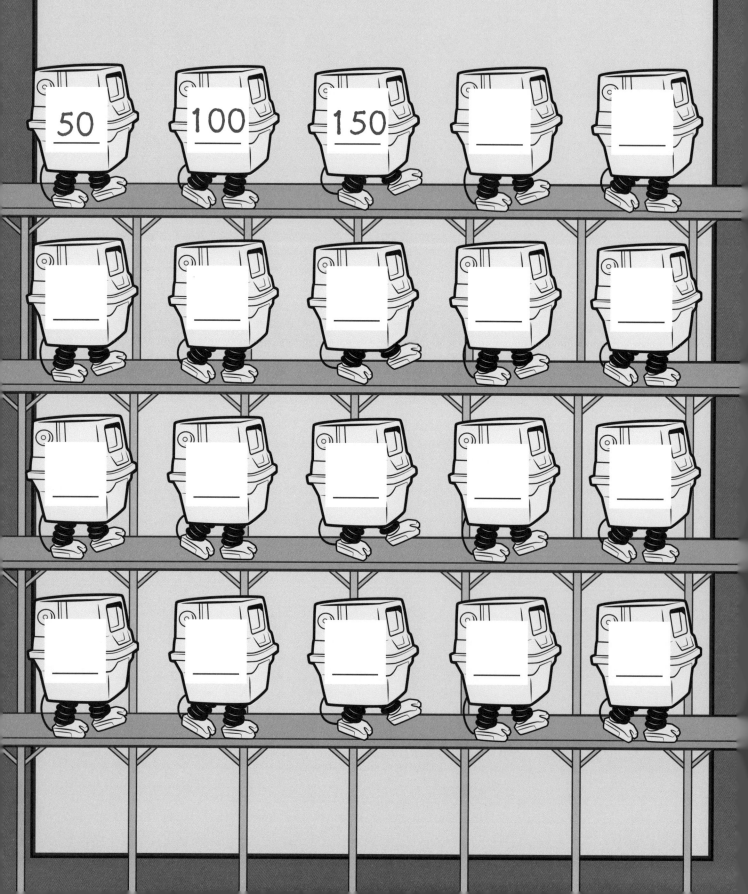

Count in Hundreds!

Fill in the missing numbers on the planets.

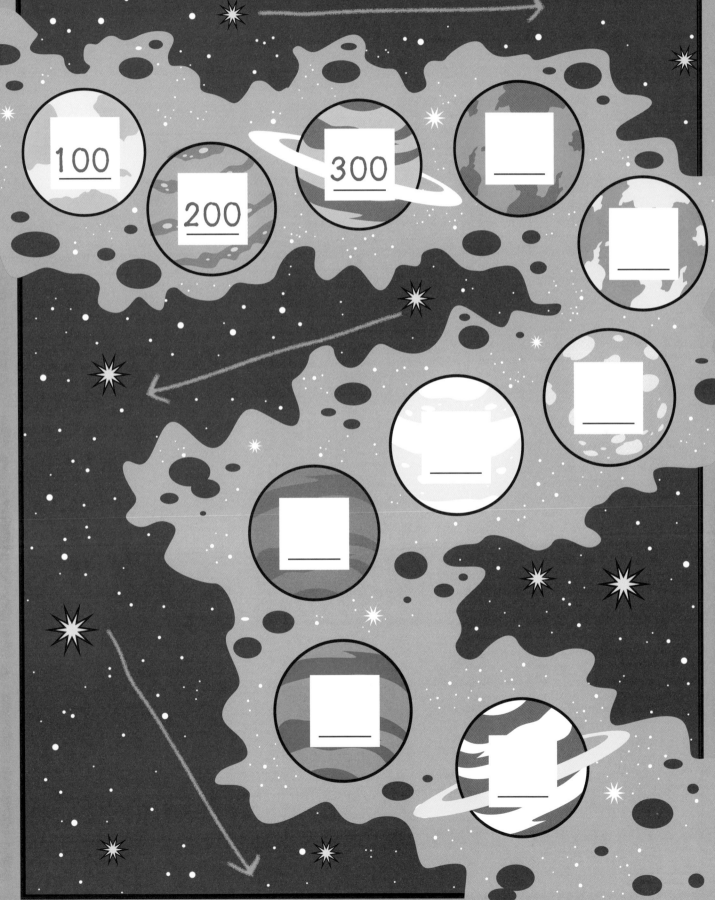

Revise Odd and Even

Count the droids on each card. Write the total in the yellow box.

Circle groups of 2 droids on each card.

If all the droids are circled, the number is **even**.
If there is a droid left over, the number is **odd**.

Colour the cards with **even** numbers in **blue**.

Colour the cards with **odd** numbers in **pink**.

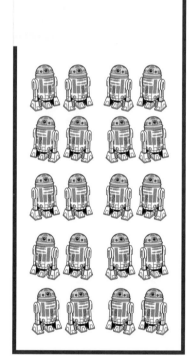

7

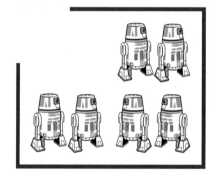

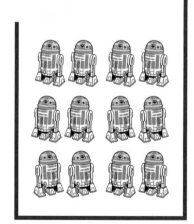

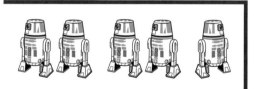

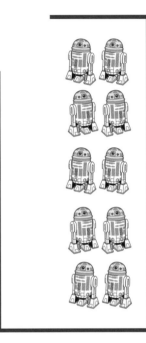

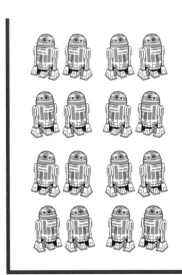

Sun Sums

Solve the equations on each sun.

If all the **sums** equal the number at the bottom, colour the sun in **yellow**.

If the **sums** do not equal the number at the bottom, colour the sun in **red**.

$70 + 2 =$ ____

$20 + 6 =$ ____

$40 + 4 =$ ____

$60 + 2 =$ ____

80

$50 + 50 =$ ____

$70 + 30 =$ ____

$20 + 80 =$ ____

$30 + 70 =$ ____

100

$36 + 4 =$ ____

$12 + 28 =$ ____

$23 + 17 =$ ____

$8 + 32 =$ ____

40

46 + 55 = ____

40 + 111 = ____

88 + 23 = ____

22 + 99 = ____

111

130 + 10 = ____

40 + 111 = ____

60 + 70 = ____

22 + 120 = ____

140

100 + 20 = ____

42 + 78 = ____

93 + 27 = ____

60 + 60 = ____

120

30 + 30 = ____

12 + 48 = ____

42 + 42 = ____

32 + 27 = ____

60

Add 10

Add the numbers in each number sentence.
Write the **sum** on the line.

6 + 10 = <u>16</u>

10 + 10 = ___

56 + 10 = ___

33 + 10 = ___

900 + 10 = ___

124 + 10 = ___

157 + 10 = ___

235 + 10 = ___

868 + 10 = ___

544 + 10 = ___

667 + 10 = ___

212 + 10 = ___

345 + 10 = ___

Add 100

Add the numbers in each number sentence.
Write the **sum** on the line.

100 + 100 = <u>200</u>

139 + 100 = ___

236 + 100 = ___

445 + 100 = ___

685 + 100 = ___

899 + 100 = ___

711 + 100 = _____

600 + 100 = _____

533 + 100 = _____

406 + 100 = _____

871 + 100 = _____

395 + 100 = _____

319 + 100 = _____

800 + 100 = _____

668 + 100 = _____

Tic-Tac-Total

Add each set of numbers. To win, draw a line through the three sums that are the same.

21 + 15	22 + 13	23 + 16
11 + 6	20 + 15	12 + 6
10 + 3	21 + 14	18 + 1

10 + 6	23 + 14	14 + 3
16 + 21	13 + 3	20 + 15
10 + 29	24 + 4	15 + 1

26 + 21	13 + 4	21 + 5
10 + 9	22 + 4	12 + 5
20 + 6	10 + 8	28 + 31

13 + 6	22 + 4	23 + 13
22 + 7	28 + 1	20 + 9
15 + 21	14 + 0	13 + 35

Cloud City Number Families

Addition facts can help you solve **subtraction** problems.
It helps to think about **number families**.

All the **equations** in this family equal 6.

6

$4 + 2 = 6$ $2 + 4 = 6$

$6 - 2 = 4$ $6 - 4 = 2$

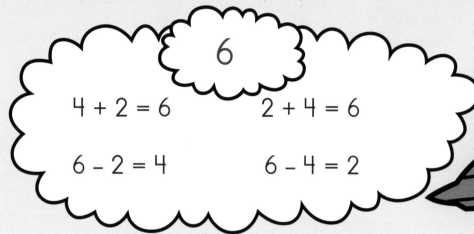

Finish the **number families**. Write the missing numbers.

12

$4 + 8 = \underline{12}$ $8 + \underline{} = 12$

$12 - \underline{} = 4$ $12 - 4 = \underline{}$

14

$5 + 9 = \underline{}$ $\underline{} + 5 = 14$

$14 - \underline{} = 5$ $14 - 5 = \underline{}$

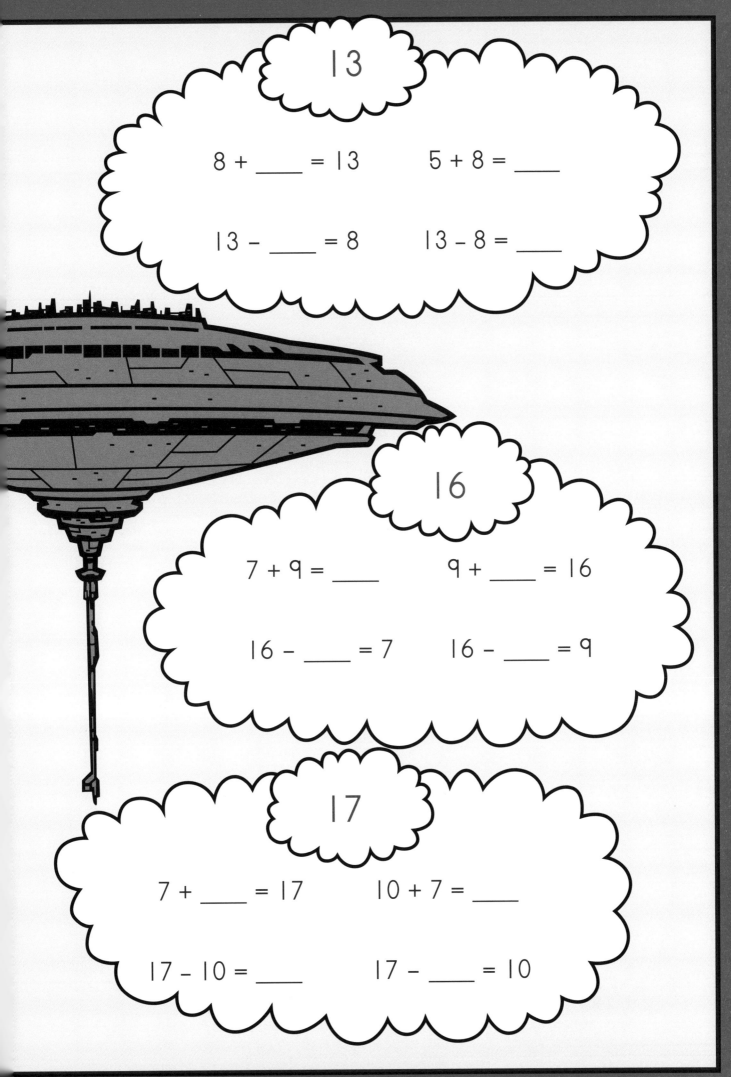

13

8 + ___ = 13   5 + 8 = ___

13 – ___ = 8   13 – 8 = ___

16

7 + 9 = ___   9 + ___ = 16

16 – ___ = 7   16 – ___ = 9

17

7 + ___ = 17   10 + 7 = ___

17 – 10 = ___   17 – ___ = 10

Lunar Subtraction

Solve the **equations** on each moon.

If all the **differences** equal the number at the bottom, colour the moon in **orange**.

If all the **differences** do not equal the number at the bottom, colour the moon in **blue**.

$11 - 1 =$ _____

$15 - 5 =$ _____

$20 - 10 =$ _____

$12 - 2 =$ _____

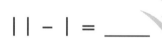

10

$19 - 8 =$ _____

$20 - 10 =$ _____

$15 - 4 =$ _____

$11 - 0 =$ _____

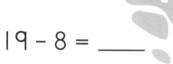

11

$10 - 5 =$ _____

$15 - 10 =$ _____

$8 - 3 =$ _____

$9 - 4 =$ _____

5

16 − 0 = ____

19 − 3 = ____

18 − 2 = ____

17 − 1 = ____

16

12 − 0 = ____

15 − 3 = ____

13 − 1 = ____

17 − 5 = ____

12

10 − 2 = ____

18 − 8 = ____

12 − 2 = ____

8 − 0 = ____

8

1 − 0 = ____

17 − 16 = ____

2 − 1 = ____

6 − 5 = ____

1

Subtract 10

Subtract the numbers in each number sentence.
Write the **difference** on the line.

20 - 10 = <u>10</u>

10 - 10 = ___

34 - 10 = ___

16 - 10 = ___

595 - 10 = ___

398 - 10 = ___

$$110 - 10 = \underline{}$$

$$165 - 10 = \underline{}$$

$$390 - 10 = \underline{}$$

$$277 - 10 = \underline{}$$

$$817 - 10 = \underline{}$$

$$444 - 10 = \underline{}$$

$$880 - 10 = \underline{}$$

$$731 - 10 = \underline{}$$

$$695 - 10 = \underline{}$$

Subtract 100

Subtract the numbers in each number sentence.
Write the **difference** on the line.

200 – 100 = _____

450 – 100 = _____

848 – 100 = _____

400 – 100 = _____

375 – 100 = _____

555 – 100 = _____

399 – 100 = _____

501 − 100 = _____

660 − 100 = _____

716 − 100 = _____

817 − 100 = _____

103 − 100 = _____

286 − 100 = _____

350 − 100 = _____

499 − 100 = _____

Tic-Subtract-Toe

Subtract each set of numbers. To win, draw a line through the three differences that are the same.

28 − 2	18 − 4	31 − 21
27 − 1	29 − 11	25 − 15
21 − 10	15 − 4	23 − 12

15 − 2	19 − 5	27 − 5
26 − 13	25 − 3	28 − 12
28 − 15	39 − 25	30 − 10

27 −20	26 −12	19 − 8
24 − 1	19 −12	29 − 18
27 − 11	24 − 12	38 − 31

23 − 10	30 − 10	19 − 3
26 − 13	23 − 21	28 − 12
23 − 20	39 − 8	17 − 1

Colourful Surprise

Add or **subtract.** Then use the key to colour in the spaces.

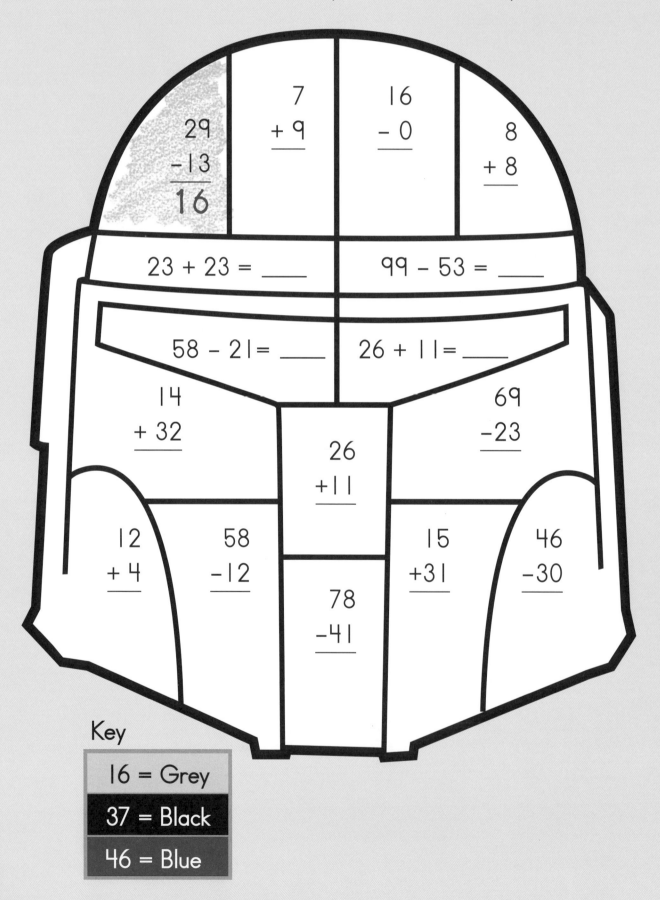

$$29 - 13 = 16$$

$$7 + 9$$

$$16 - 0$$

$$8 + 8$$

$$23 + 23 = \underline{}$$

$$99 - 53 = \underline{}$$

$$58 - 21 = \underline{}$$

$$26 + 11 = \underline{}$$

$$14 + 32$$

$$69 - 23$$

$$26 + 11$$

$$12 + 4$$

$$58 - 12$$

$$15 + 31$$

$$46 - 30$$

$$78 - 41$$

Key

16 = Grey

37 = Black

46 = Blue

$$11 + 12$$

$$22 + 1$$

$$89 - 42$$

$$13 + 10$$

$$58 - 35$$

$$31 + 16$$

$$46 + 13 = \underline{\quad}$$

$$89 - 30 = \underline{\quad}$$

$$23 + 0$$

$$99 - 76$$

$$98 - 51$$

$$20 + 3 = \underline{\quad}$$

$$26 + 21$$

$$31 + 16 = \underline{\quad}$$

$$99 - 52$$

$$33 - 10$$

$$26 + 21$$

Key

23 = Red

47 = Black

59 = Yellow

Break the Code

Add or **subtract**.

Use your answers to decode the riddle.

$$\begin{array}{r} 10 \\ + 24 \\ \hline \end{array}$$

A

$$\begin{array}{r} 29 \\ - 23 \\ \hline \end{array}$$

D

$$\begin{array}{r} 24 \\ + 31 \\ \hline \end{array}$$

E

$$\begin{array}{r} 63 \\ - 21 \\ \hline \end{array}$$

G

$$\begin{array}{r} 52 \\ - 20 \\ \hline \end{array}$$

H

$$\begin{array}{r} 85 \\ + 14 \\ \hline \end{array}$$

I

$$\begin{array}{r} 65 \\ + 11 \\ \hline \end{array}$$

K

$$\begin{array}{r} 94 \\ - 23 \\ \hline \end{array}$$

O

$$\begin{array}{r} 70 \\ + 7 \\ \hline \end{array}$$

R

$$\begin{array}{r} 24 \\ - 13 \\ \hline \end{array}$$

S

$$\begin{array}{r} 41 \\ + 57 \\ \hline \end{array}$$

T

Riddle:

Why did Darth Vader cross the road?

Answer:

$\overline{}$ $\overline{}$ $\quad$ $\overline{}$ $\overline{}$ $\overline{}$ $\quad$ $\overline{}$ $\overline{}$ $\quad$ $\overline{}$ $\overline{}$ $\overline{}$
98　71　　42　55　98　　98　71　　98　32　55

$\qquad$ $\overline{}$ $\overline{}$ $\overline{}$ $\overline{}$ $\quad$ $\overline{}$ $\overline{}$ $\overline{}$ $\overline{}$
　　6　34　77　76　　11　99　6　55

Luke's Dinner

Add or **subtract**.

Use your answers to decode the riddle.

$\begin{array}{r} 78 \\ -\ 20 \\ \hline \end{array}$	$\begin{array}{r} 74 \\ +\ 24 \\ \hline \end{array}$	$\begin{array}{r} 82 \\ -\ 41 \\ \hline \end{array}$	$\begin{array}{r} 55 \\ +\ 24 \\ \hline \end{array}$
E	F	H	K

$\begin{array}{r} 64 \\ -\ 51 \\ \hline \end{array}$	$\begin{array}{r} 12 \\ +\ 75 \\ \hline \end{array}$	$\begin{array}{r} 33 \\ +\ 45 \\ \hline \end{array}$	$\begin{array}{r} 89 \\ -\ 53 \\ \hline \end{array}$
L	O	R	S

$\begin{array}{r} 64 \\ -\ 52 \\ \hline \end{array}$	$\begin{array}{r} 53 \\ +\ 41 \\ \hline \end{array}$
T	U

Riddle:

What did Yoda say when Luke tried
to eat his dinner with a spoon?

Answer:

___ ___ ___   ___ ___ ___
94 36 58   12 41 58

___ ___ ___ ___ ,   ___ ___ ___ ___ .
98 87 78 79   13 94 79 58

Baby Jawa

Add to find the **sums**.

Use your answers to decode the riddle.

$$35 + 8$$

A

$$28 + 25$$

C

$$64 + 19$$

D

$$36 + 8$$

L

$$57 + 16$$

N

$$58 + 37$$

R

$$41 + 29$$

E

$$23 + 68$$

S

$$78 + 18$$

W

Riddle:

What do you call a baby Jawa?

Answer:

| 43 | 91 | 43 | 73 | 83 | 53 | 95 | 43 | 96 | 44 | 70 | 95 |

Yoda's Garden

Add to find the **sums**.

Use your answers to decode the riddle.

$16 + 36$

B

$41 + 29$

E

$26 + 9$

F

$36 + 7$

H

$55 + 6$

I

$69 + 28$

M

$53 + 19$

N

$35 + 45$

G

$73 + 18$

S

$38 + 22$

T

$44 + 27$

R

$77 + 7$

A

Riddle:

Why is Yoda such a good gardener?

Answer:

	43	70		43	84	91				
80	71	70	70	72		35	61	72	80	70	71	91

Subtraction Bingo

Subtract to find the **differences**.

Colour in the cards with answers that
match Darth Maul's card.

48

52
− 16

70
− 22

66
− 18

92
− 58

80
− 32

97
− 48

25
− 8

74
− 26

83
− 27

83
− 35

38 − 19	77 − 19	32 − 13	44 − 27
98 − 39	67 − 19	64 − 59	82 − 49
23 − 15	73 − 25	43 − 39	54 − 7
53 − 5	55 − 38	87 − 39	95 − 19

Maths Matchmaker

Subtract to find the **differences**.

The answer on each card has a matching answer on a second card.

Colour in each pair of answers with the same colour.

$$62 - 53$$

$$53 - 14$$

$$41 - 28$$

$$21 - 17$$

$$64 - 57$$

$$40 - 12$$

$$37 - 8$$

$$72 - 65$$

$$81 - 35$$

$$62 - 23$$

$$70 - 27$$

$$52 - 24$$

$$90 - 86$$

$$48 - 19$$

$$93 - 47$$

$$33 - 16$$

$$46 - 29$$

$$22 - 13$$

$$50 - 37$$

$$80 - 37$$

How Many 4s?

Add to find the **sums**.

Colour in the cards that have 4 ones in the answer.

36 + 10	54 + 20	60 + 4
29 + 23	71 + 9	56 + 38

18 + 16	42 + 32	39 + 51	32 + 28
85 + 9	15 + 28	25 + 40	62 + 22

Look for the 9s!

Subtract to find the **differences**.

Colour in the cards that have 9 ones in the answer.

$$\begin{array}{r} 98 \\ -19 \\ \hline \end{array}$$

$$\begin{array}{r} 76 \\ -67 \\ \hline \end{array}$$

$$\begin{array}{r} 97 \\ -77 \\ \hline \end{array}$$

$$\begin{array}{r} 55 \\ -38 \\ \hline \end{array}$$

$$\begin{array}{r} 80 \\ -16 \\ \hline \end{array}$$

$$\begin{array}{r} 67 \\ -58 \\ \hline \end{array}$$

$$\begin{array}{r} 74 \\ -35 \\ \hline \end{array}$$

$$\begin{array}{r} 42 \\ -33 \\ \hline \end{array}$$

$$\begin{array}{r} 77 \\ -28 \\ \hline \end{array}$$

$$\begin{array}{r} 45 \\ -19 \\ \hline \end{array}$$

$$\begin{array}{r} 94 \\ -68 \\ \hline \end{array}$$

$$\begin{array}{r} 68 \\ -39 \\ \hline \end{array}$$

$$\begin{array}{r} 41 \\ -33 \\ \hline \end{array}$$

$$\begin{array}{r} 40 \\ -21 \\ \hline \end{array}$$

Maths Concentration

Add or **subtract**.

Colour in the two cards on this page that have matching answers.

$$36 + 35$$

$$76 - 57$$

$$43 - 36$$

$$98 - 89$$

$$27 + 64$$

$$13 + 29$$

$$81 - 69$$

$$63 + 9$$

$$61 - 19$$

Add or **subtract**.

Colour in the two cards on this page that have matching answers.

83
− 26
___

49
+ 13
___

91
− 56
___

50
− 33
___

45
+ 45
___

14
+ 68
___

90
− 44
___

16
+ 18
___

19
− 16
___

17
+ 18
___

Word Problems

Read each word problem.

Decide if you need to **add** or **subtract**.

Write the **number sentence**.

Write the answer in the yellow box.

Han Solo read 25 pages of his book yesterday.

He read 18 pages today.

How many pages did he read altogether?

_____

Mace Windu wants to give a lightsaber to every Padawan.

If he has 30 lightsabers and there are 46 Padawans, how many more lightsabers does he need?

_____

15 Jedi are waiting in a line. Obi-Wan Kenobi is tenth in line. How many Jedi are behind Obi-Wan?

_____

Luke Skywalker is looking for Darth Vader in starfighters.

He searched 11 X-wings and 13 vulture droids.

How many starfighters did he search altogether?

_____

The band has 4 human musicians and 7 alien musicians.

Does the band have more human musicians or alien musicians?

_____

How many more?

_____

There were 37 sandwiches on a table.

Anakin ate 10 sandwiches and Padmé ate 4 sandwiches.

How many sandwiches did they eat?

_____

How many sandwiches are left?

_____

Hundreds of Stars

Add to find the **sums.**

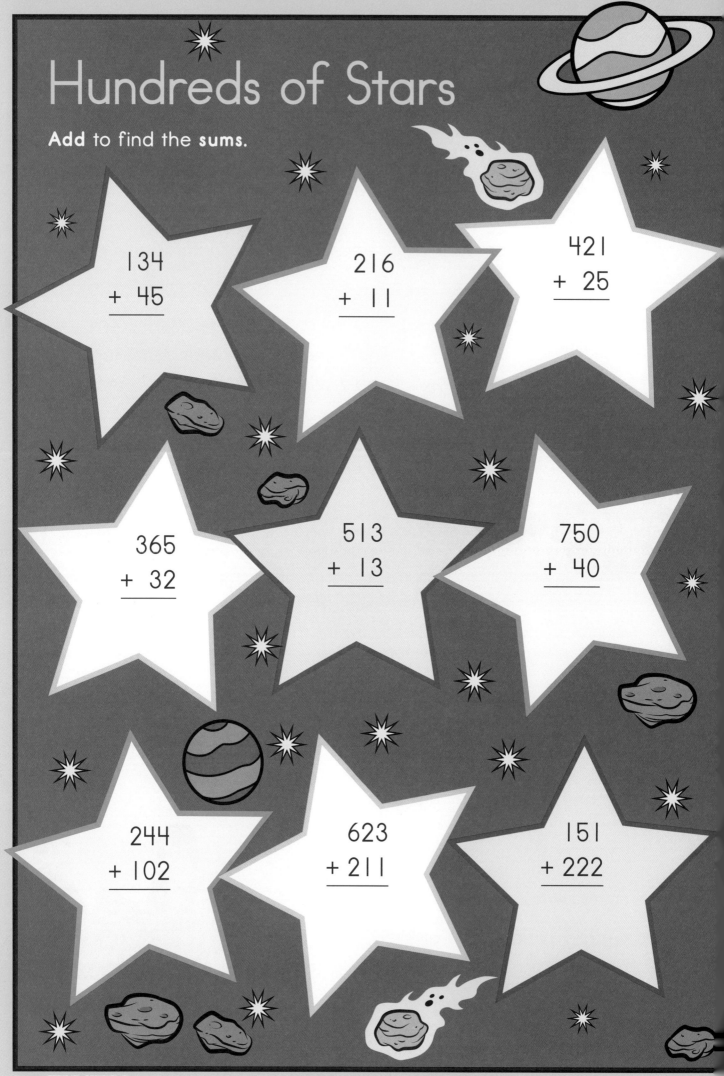

134
+ 45

216
+ 11

421
+ 25

365
+ 32

513
+ 13

750
+ 40

244
+ 102

623
+ 211

151
+ 222

Subtract to find the **differences.**

556
- 3

862
- 11

688
- 64

964
- 22

468
- 51

759
- 19

473
- 132

848
- 212

287
- 166

Revise Arrays

An **array** is a set of things arranged into equal groups.

Instead of counting objects one by one, you can put the objects into equal groups and count the groups.

Here is an **array** of 6 Death Stars.

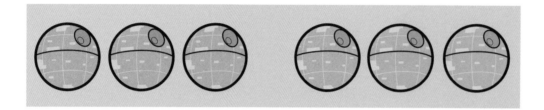

Here is another **array** of 6 Death Stars.

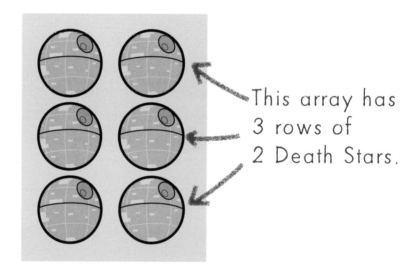

This array has 3 rows of 2 Death Stars.

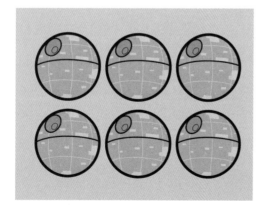

Here is another **array** of 6 Death Stars.

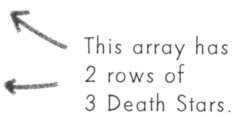

This array has 2 rows of 3 Death Stars.

Here is an **array** of 8 Death Stars.

Draw another array of 8 Death Stars.

Can you draw one more array of 8 Death Stars?

Planet Arrays

Here is an **array** of 12 planets.

Draw at least two more arrays of 12 planets.

Here is an **array** of 18 planets.

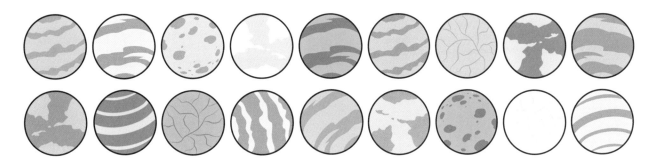

Draw at least two more arrays of 18 planets.

Repeated Addition

Each of the coloured card groupings has the same number of Gungans.

Write how many Gungans and how many cards are in each grouping.

Then write the **repeated addition sentence**.

There are ___4___ Gungans on each card.

There are ___3___ cards.

4 + 4 + 4 = 12

There are _____ Gungans on each card.

There are _____ cards.

_____

There are _____ Gungans on each card.

There are _____ cards.

_____

There are _____ Gungans on each card.

There are _____ cards.

_____

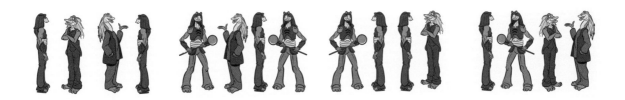

There are _____ Gungans on each card.

There are _____ cards.

_____

Groups of Banthas

Finish the **addition** sentences.

$$2 + 2 + \underline{2} + \underline{2} = \underline{8}$$

$$4 + \underline{} = \underline{}$$

5 + ___ + ___ + ___ = ___

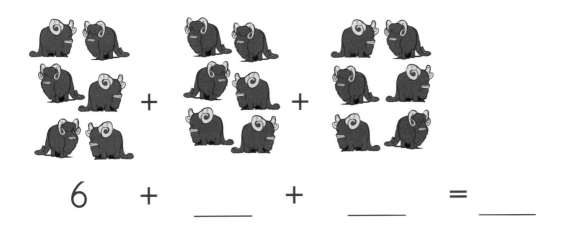

6 + ___ + ___ = ___

3 + ___ + ___ + ___ + ___ = ___

Matching Creatures

Solve each **number sentence**.

The answer on each creature has a matching answer on a second creature.

Colour each pair of creatures with the same colour.

1 + 1 + 1 + 1 = _____

3
3
3
+ 3
___

8 + 8 = _____

4 + 4 + 4 + 4 = _____

12
+12
___

6
+ 6
___

$5 + 5 + 5 + 5 + 5 + 5 =$ ___

$8 + 8 + 8 =$ ___

$2 + 2 =$ ___

$10 + 10 + 10 =$ ___

$5 + 5 =$ ___

$2 + 2 + 2 + 2 + 2 =$ ___

Word Problems

Read each word problem. Write the **number sentence** on the line.

Write the answer in the yellow box.

Anakin has 4 bags of droid parts.
There are 6 droid parts in each bag.
How many droid parts does Anakin have?

$$6 + 6 + 6 + 6 = \quad 24$$

Obi-Wan is putting lightsabers into cabinets.
Each cabinet holds 5 lightsabers.
Obi-Wan filled 4 cabinets.
How many lightsabers did he put away?

_____

Padmé is giving 1 robe to each of her 8 handmaidens.
How many robes does Padmé need?

_____

Droids are sold in boxes with 3 droids in each box.
If Luke bought 5 boxes, how many droids did
he buy altogether?

_____

Chewbacca and Han have to paint 6 rooms.
Each room needs 2 cans of paint. How many cans
of paint do they need to do all 6 rooms?

_____

Each dewback needs to drink 2 buckets of
water every day. How many buckets of water
are needed for 4 dewbacks every day?

_____

Aayla Secura can defeat 3 clone troopers every minute.
How many clone troopers can she defeat in 6 minutes?

_____

$\frac{1}{2}$ Is One Half

Fractions show parts of a whole.
They can be written in words (**one half**)
or as a figure ($\frac{1}{2}$).

Colour in **one half** of each shape.

Write the **fraction** in the space you coloured.

How many halves does each shape have? _____

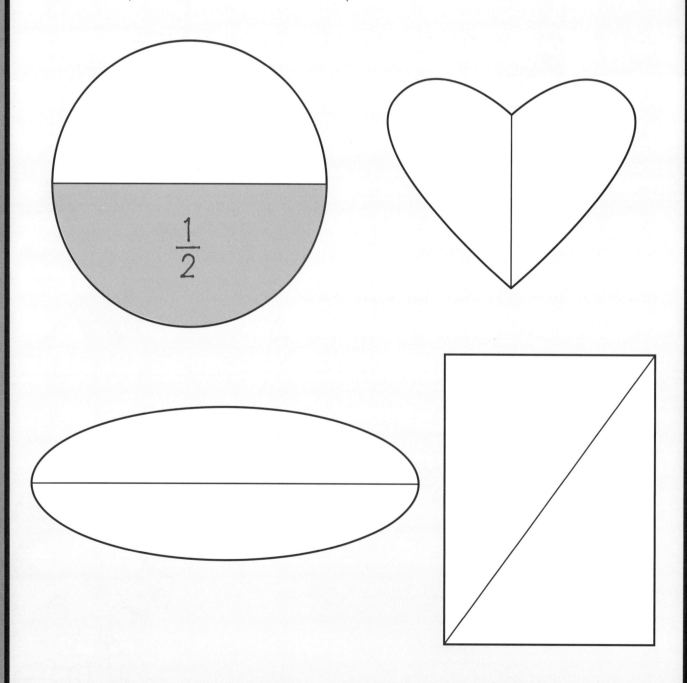

¼ Is One Quarter

Colour in **one quarter** of each shape.

Write the **fraction** in the space you coloured.

How many quarters does each shape have? _____

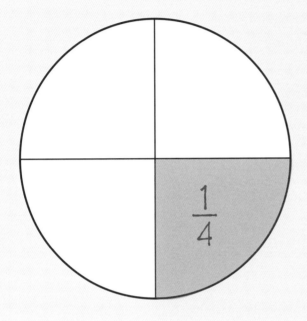

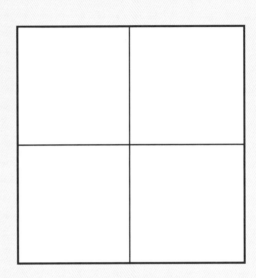

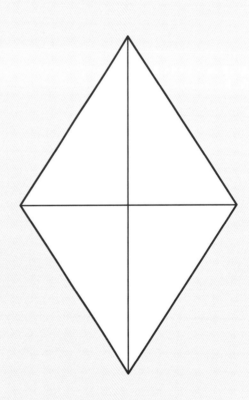

$\frac{1}{3}$ Is One Third

Colour in **one third** of each shape.

Write the **fraction** in the space you coloured.

How many thirds does each shape have? _____

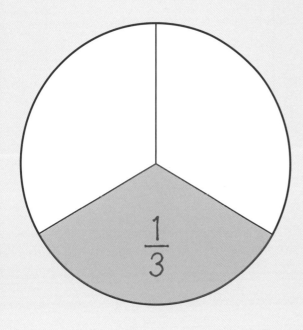

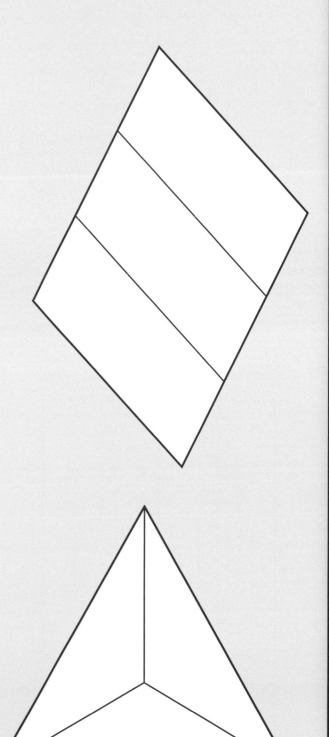

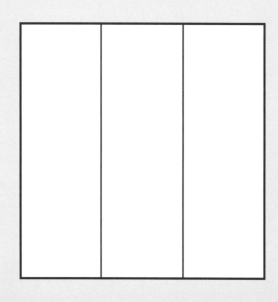

$\frac{1}{6}$ Is One Sixth

Colour in **one sixth** of each shape.

Write the **fraction** in the space you coloured.

How many sixths does each shape have? _____

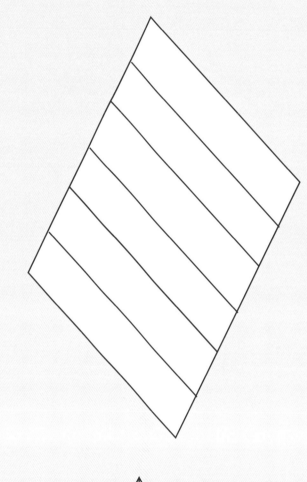

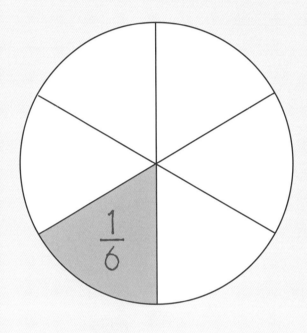

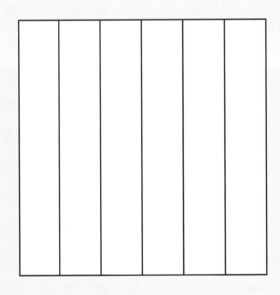

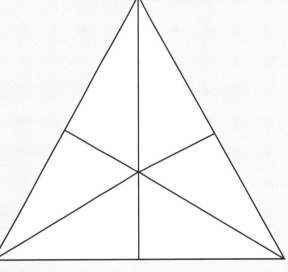

Planetary Fractions

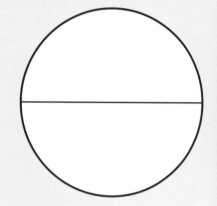
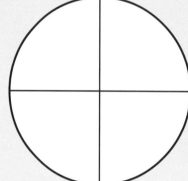

Colour in the **fractions**.

Colour $\frac{2}{3}$ **blue**.

Colour $\frac{3}{4}$ **red**.

Colour $\frac{1}{2}$ **brown**.

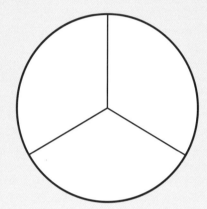

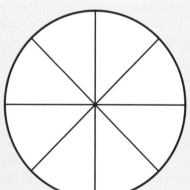
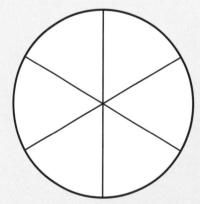
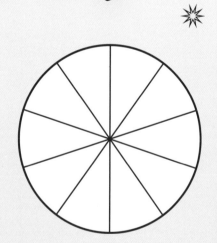

Colour $\frac{5}{8}$ **green**.

Colour $\frac{3}{6}$ **purple**.

Colour $\frac{7}{10}$ **orange**.

Matching Fractions

Write the **fraction** on the line.

Draw a line between the **fractions** that are the same.

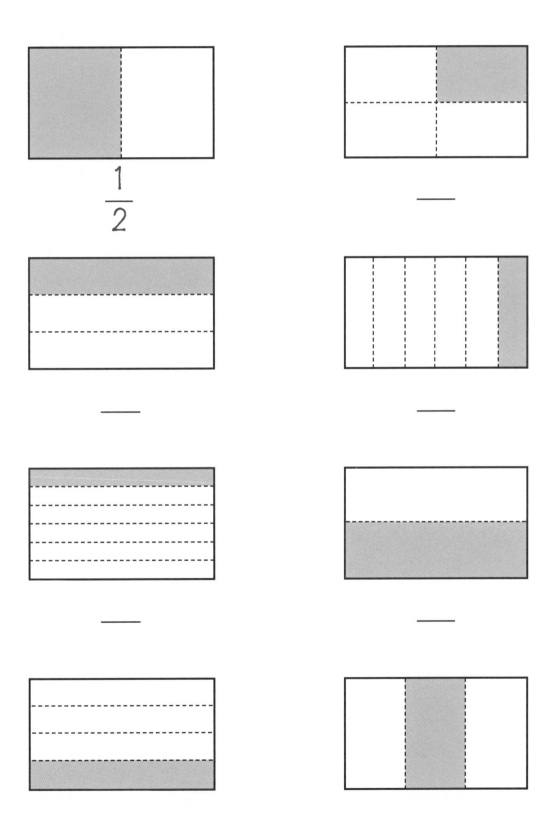

A Piece of Planet

Draw a line from the **fraction** to the matching shape.

$\dfrac{1}{2}$

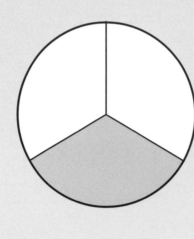

$\dfrac{1}{3}$

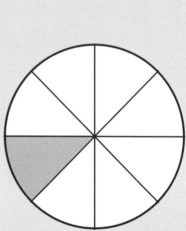

$\dfrac{1}{4}$

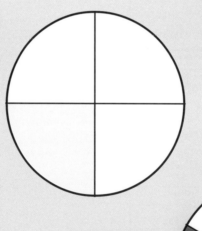

$\dfrac{1}{6}$

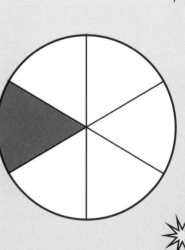

$\dfrac{1}{8}$

What Fraction?

Read each word problem.
Write the answer in words on the line.
Write the answer as a **fraction** in the box.

Leia cut her apple in half.

If she eats one piece of the apple, how much will she have left to give to Luke?

_____ _____

Chewbacca cut a sandwich in thirds.

If he eats one piece of the sandwich, what fraction of the sandwich did he eat?

_____

_____

Yoda cut a pie into four equal pieces. If he eats one piece of pie, what fraction of the pie did he eat?

_____

_____

Shape Riddles

Read the clues.

Draw a line from the shape to the riddle that matches.

Write the name of the shape on the line.

circle

rhombus

triangle

square

rectangle

I have 4 straight sides.
My opposite sides are the
same length.

_____

I have 3 straight sides and 3 corners.
My angles add up to 180°.

_____

I have 4 straight sides.
I have 4 right angles.

_____

I have 4 straight sides.
My opposite sides are equal.
My opposite angles are equal.

_____

My edges are all the same
distance from my centre.
I don't have any straight lines.

_____

Same Shape

Look at the shape on each card.

Draw a matching shape on the card next to it.

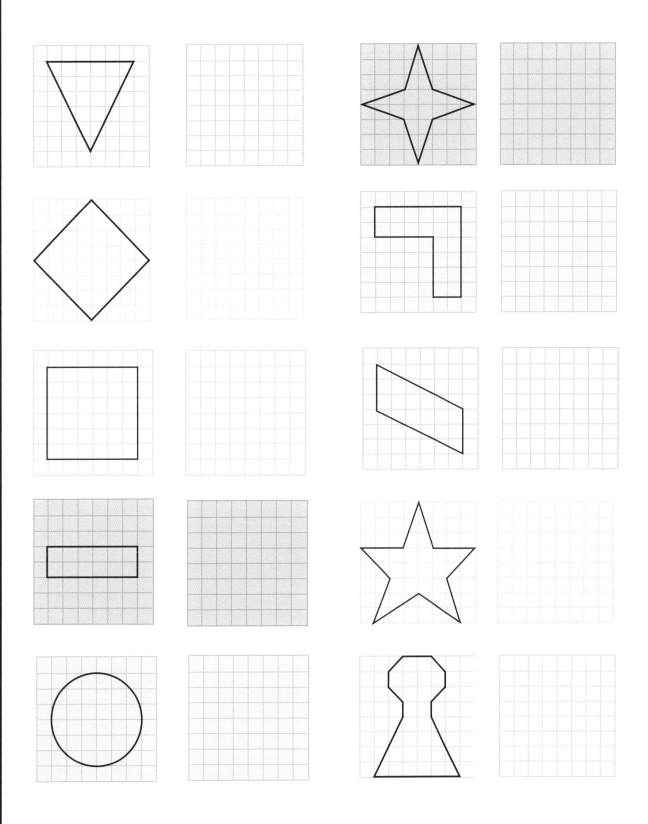

Geometry Riddles

Read the clues.

Draw a line from the 3-D shape to the matching riddle.

Write the name of the shape on the line.

cube

I have 4 rectangular and 2 square faces.
I also have 8 corners and 12 edges.

_____

cone

I have 6 square faces all the same.
I also have 8 corners and 12 edges.

_____

square-based pyramid

I have only 1 face and it is curved.

_____

I have a circle as my base,
and a curved face and point.

_____

cuboid

I have 1 square face.
I have 4 triangular faces.

_____

sphere

Answers

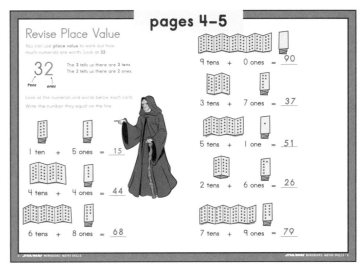

Revise Place Value

You can use **place value** to work out how much numerals are worth. Look at **32**.

32

tens ones

The 3 tells us there are 3 tens.
The 2 tells us there are 2 ones.

Look at the numerals and words below each card. Write the number they equal on the line.

1 ten + 5 ones = 15
4 tens + 4 ones = 44
6 tens + 8 ones = 68

9 tens + 0 ones = 90
3 tens + 7 ones = 37
5 tens + 1 one = 51
2 tens + 6 ones = 26
7 tens + 9 ones = 79

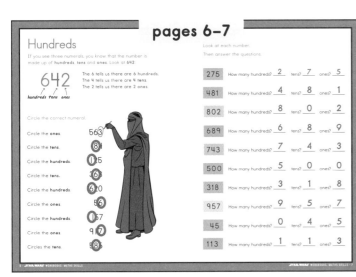

Hundreds

If you see three numerals, you know that the number is made up of **hundreds**, **tens** and **ones**. Look at **642**.

642

hundreds tens ones

The 6 tells us there are 6 hundreds.
The 4 tells us there are 4 tens.
The 2 tells us there are 2 ones.

Circle the correct numeral.

Circle the **ones**. 563
Circle the **tens**. 481
Circle the **hundreds**. 125
Circle the **tens**. 763
Circle the **hundreds**. 620
Circle the **ones**. 56
Circle the **hundreds**. 157
Circle the **ones**. 917
Circles the **tens**. 585

Look at each number. Then answer the questions.

275 How many hundreds? 2 tens? 7 ones? 5
481 How many hundreds? 4 tens? 8 ones? 1
802 How many hundreds? 8 tens? 0 ones? 2
689 How many hundreds? 6 tens? 8 ones? 9
743 How many hundreds? 7 tens? 4 ones? 3
500 How many hundreds? 5 tens? 0 ones? 0
318 How many hundreds? 3 tens? 1 ones? 8
957 How many hundreds? 9 tens? 5 ones? 7
45 How many hundreds? 0 tens? 4 ones? 5
113 How many hundreds? 1 tens? 1 ones? 3

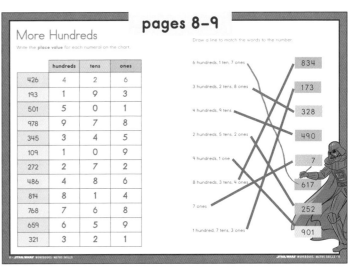

More Hundreds

Write the **place value** for each numeral on the chart.

	hundreds	tens	ones
426	4	2	6
193	1	9	3
501	5	0	1
978	9	7	8
345	3	4	5
109	1	0	9
272	2	7	2
486	4	8	6
814	8	1	4
768	7	6	8
659	6	5	9
321	3	2	1

Draw a line to match the words to the number.

6 hundreds, 1 ten, 7 ones — 617
3 hundreds, 2 tens, 8 ones — 328
4 hundreds, 9 tens — 490
2 hundreds, 5 tens, 2 ones — 252
9 hundreds, 1 one — 901
8 hundreds, 3 tens, 4 ones — 834
7 ones — 7
1 hundred, 7 tens, 3 ones — 173

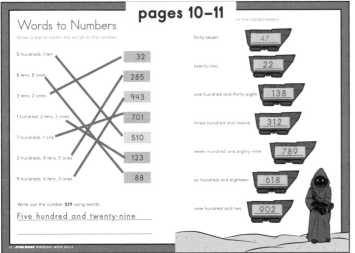

Words to Numbers

Draw a line to match the words to the number.

5 hundreds, 1 ten — 510
8 tens, 8 ones — 88
3 tens, 2 ones — 32
1 hundred, 2 tens, 3 ones — 123
7 hundreds, 1 one — 701
2 hundreds, 8 tens, 5 ones — 285
9 hundreds, 4 tens, 3 ones — 943

Write out the number **529** using words:

Five hundred and twenty-nine

...on the sandcrawlers.

forty-seven — 47
twenty-two — 22
one hundred and thirty-eight — 138
three hundred and twelve — 312
seven hundred and eighty-nine — 789
six hundred and eighteen — 618
nine hundred and two — 902

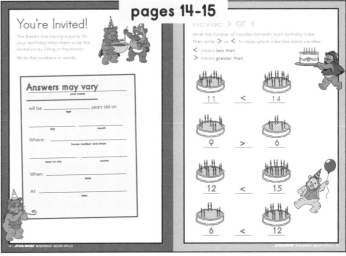

You're Invited!

The Ewoks are having a party for your birthday! Help them write the invitation by filling in the blanks. Write the numbers in words.

Answers may vary

your name

will be _____ years old on
age

_____ _____
day   month

Where: _____
house number and street

_____
town or city   county

When: _____
date

At: _____
time

Revise > or <

Write the number of candles beneath each birthday cake. Then write **>** or **<** to show which cake has more candles.

< means **less than**.
> means **greater than**.

11 < 14
9 > 6
12 < 15
6 < 12

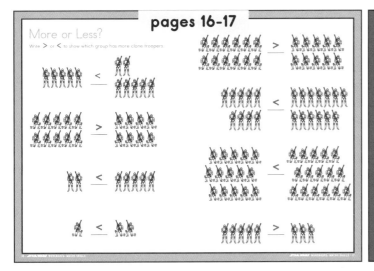

More or Less?

Write **>** or **<** to show which group has more clone troopers.

<

>

<

<

>

<

>

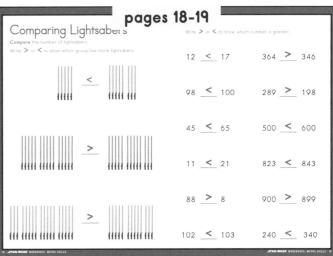

Comparing Lightsabers

Compare the number of lightsabers.
Write **>** or **<** to show which group has more lightsabers.

<

>

>

Write **>** or **<** to show which number is greater.

12 < 17   364 > 346
98 < 100   289 > 198
45 < 65   500 < 600
11 < 21   823 < 843
88 > 8   900 > 899
102 < 103   240 < 340

Answers

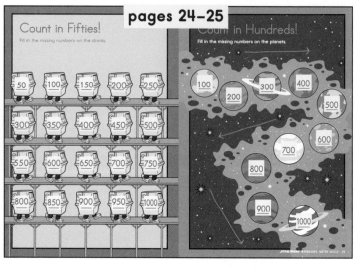

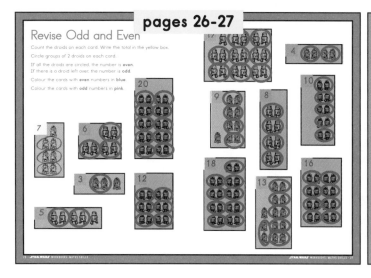

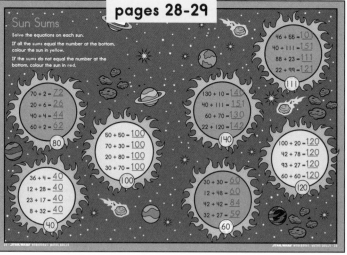

Add 10

Add the numbers in each number sentence.
Write the **sum** on the line.

6 + 10 = 16

10 + 10 = 20

56 + 10 = 66

33 + 10 = 43

900 + 10 = 910

124 + 10 = 134

157 + 10 = 167

235 + 10 = 245

868 + 10 = 878

544 + 10 = 554

667 + 10 = 677

212 + 10 = 222

345 + 10 = 355

Add 100

Add the numbers in each number sentence.
Write the **sum** on the line.

100 + 100 = 200

139 + 100 = 239

236 + 100 = 336

445 + 100 = 545

685 + 100 = 785

899 + 100 = 999

711 + 100 = 811

600 + 100 = 700

533 + 100 = 633

406 + 100 = 506

871 + 100 = 971

395 + 100 = 495

319 + 100 = 419

800 + 100 = 900

668 + 100 = 768

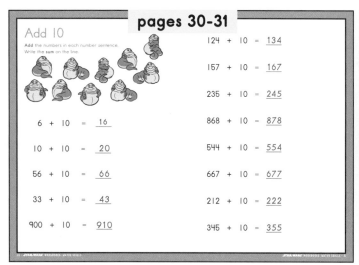
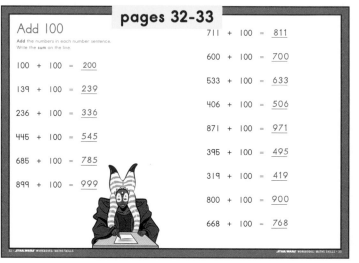

pages 34-35

pages 36-37

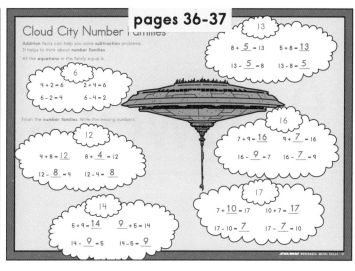

pages 38-39

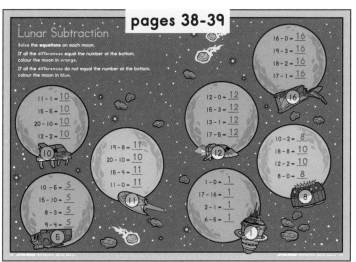

pages 40-41

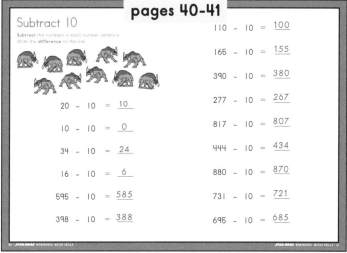

pages 42-43

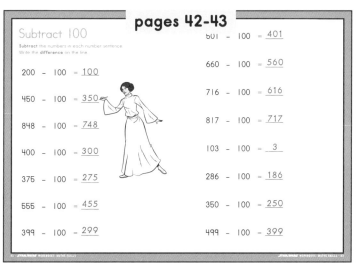

pages 44-45

pages 46-47

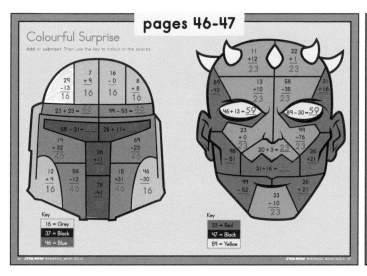

pages 48-49

Answers

pages 50–51

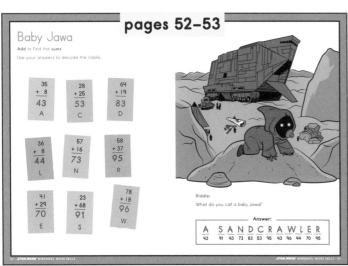

pages 52–53

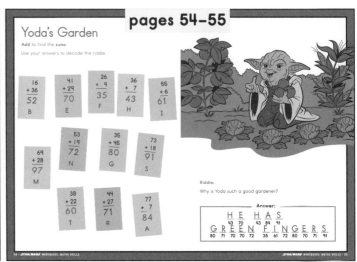

pages 54–55

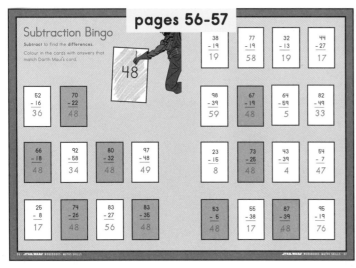

pages 56–57

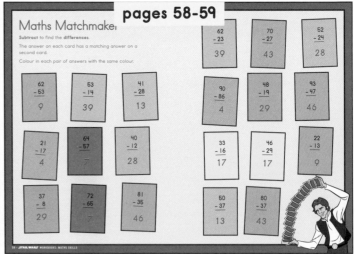

pages 58–59

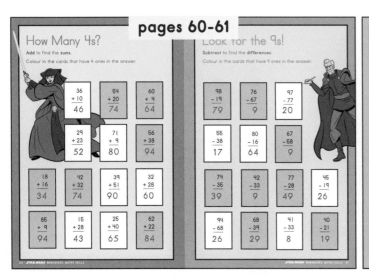

pages 60–61

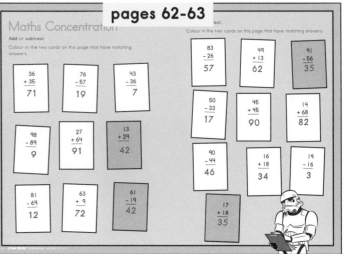

pages 62–63

Word Problems

Read each word problem.

Decide if you need to **add** or **subtract**.

Write the **number sentence**.

Write the answer in the yellow box.

Han Solo read 25 pages of his book yesterday.
He read 18 pages today.
How many pages did he read altogether?

$25 + 18 = 43$

Mace Windu wants to give a lightsaber to every Padawan.
If he has 30 lightsabers and there are 46 Padawans, how many more lightsabers does he need?

$46 - 30 = 16$

15 Jedi are waiting in a line. Obi-Wan Kenobi is tenth in line. How many Jedi are behind Obi-Wan?

$15 - 10 = 5$

Luke Skywalker is looking for Darth Vader in starfighters.
He searched 11 X-wings and 13 vulture droids.
How many starfighters did he search altogether?

$11 + 13 = 24$

The band has 4 human musicians and 7 alien musicians.
Does the band have more human musicians or alien musicians?

alien musicians

How many more?

$7 - 4 = 3$

There were 37 sandwiches on a table.
Anakin ate 10 sandwiches and Padmé ate 4 sandwiches.
How many sandwiches did they eat?

$10 + 4 = 14$

How many sandwiches are left?

$37 - 14 = 23$

Hundreds of Stars

Add to find the sums. Subtract to find the differences.

$\begin{array}{r} 134 \\ + 45 \\ \hline 179 \end{array}$ $\begin{array}{r} 216 \\ + 11 \\ \hline 227 \end{array}$ $\begin{array}{r} 421 \\ + 25 \\ \hline 446 \end{array}$ $\begin{array}{r} 556 \\ - 3 \\ \hline 553 \end{array}$ $\begin{array}{r} 862 \\ - 11 \\ \hline 851 \end{array}$ $\begin{array}{r} 688 \\ - 64 \\ \hline 624 \end{array}$

$\begin{array}{r} 365 \\ + 32 \\ \hline 397 \end{array}$ $\begin{array}{r} 513 \\ + 13 \\ \hline 526 \end{array}$ $\begin{array}{r} 750 \\ + 40 \\ \hline 790 \end{array}$ $\begin{array}{r} 964 \\ - 22 \\ \hline 942 \end{array}$ $\begin{array}{r} 468 \\ - 51 \\ \hline 417 \end{array}$ $\begin{array}{r} 759 \\ - 19 \\ \hline 740 \end{array}$

$\begin{array}{r} 244 \\ + 102 \\ \hline 346 \end{array}$ $\begin{array}{r} 623 \\ + 211 \\ \hline 834 \end{array}$ $\begin{array}{r} 151 \\ + 222 \\ \hline 373 \end{array}$ $\begin{array}{r} 473 \\ - 132 \\ \hline 341 \end{array}$ $\begin{array}{r} 848 \\ - 212 \\ \hline 636 \end{array}$ $\begin{array}{r} 287 \\ - 166 \\ \hline 121 \end{array}$

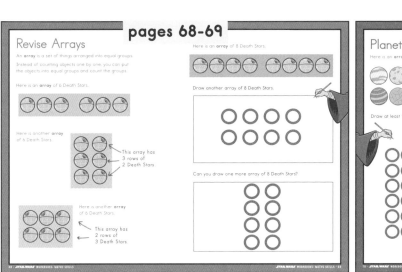

Revise Arrays

An **array** is a set of things arranged into equal groups.

Instead of counting objects one by one, you can put the objects into equal groups and count the groups.

Here is an **array** of 6 Death Stars.

Here is another **array** of 6 Death Stars.

This array has 3 rows of 2 Death Stars.

Here is another **array** of 6 Death Stars.

This array has 2 rows of 3 Death Stars.

Here is an **array** of 8 Death Stars.

Draw another array of 8 Death Stars.

Can you draw one more array of 8 Death Stars?

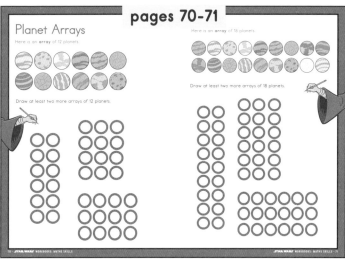

Planet Arrays

Here is an **array** of 12 planets.

Draw at least two more arrays of 12 planets.

Here is an **array** of 18 planets.

Draw at least two more arrays of 18 planets.

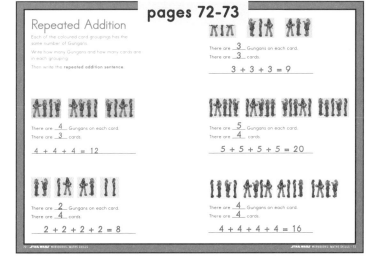

Repeated Addition

Each of the coloured card groupings has the same number of Gungans.

Write how many Gungans and how many cards are in each grouping.

Then write the **repeated addition sentence**.

There are **4** Gungans on each card.
There are **3** cards.

$4 + 4 + 4 = 12$

There are **2** Gungans on each card.
There are **4** cards.

$2 + 2 + 2 + 2 = 8$

There are **3** Gungans on each card.
There are **3** cards.

$3 + 3 + 3 = 9$

There are **5** Gungans on each card.
There are **4** cards.

$5 + 5 + 5 + 5 = 20$

There are **4** Gungans on each card.
There are **4** cards.

$4 + 4 + 4 + 4 = 16$

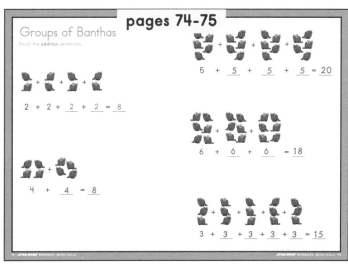

Groups of Banthas

Finish the **addition** sentences.

$2 + 2 + 2 + 2 = 8$

$4 + 4 = 8$

$5 + 5 + 5 + 5 = 20$

$6 + 6 + 6 = 18$

$3 + 3 + 3 + 3 + 3 = 15$

Matching Creatures

Solve each **number sentence**.

The answer on each creature has a matching answer on a second creature.

Colour each pair of creatures with the same colour.

$5 + 5 + 5 + 5 + 5 + 5 = 30$

$3 + 3 + 3 + 3 = 12$

$1 + 1 + 1 + 1 = 4$

$8 + 8 + 8 = 24$

$4 + 4 + 4 + 4 = 16$

$8 + 8 = 16$

$2 + 2 + 2 + 2 = 8$

$10 + 10 + 10 = 30$

$12 + 12 = 24$

$6 + 6 = 12$

$5 + 5 = ?$

$2 + 2 + 2 + 2 = ?$

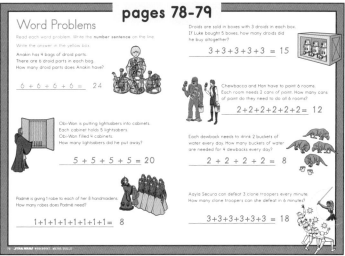

Word Problems

Read each word problem. Write the **number sentence** on the line.

Write the answer in the yellow box.

Anakin has 4 bags of droid parts.
There are 6 droid parts in each bag.
How many droid parts does Anakin have?

$6 + 6 + 6 + 6 = 24$

Obi-Wan is putting lightsabers into cabinets.
Each cabinet holds 5 lightsabers.
Obi-Wan filled 4 cabinets.
How many lightsabers did he put away?

$5 + 5 + 5 + 5 = 20$

Padmé is giving 1 robe to each of her 8 handmaidens.
How many robes does Padmé need?

$1 + 1 + 1 + 1 + 1 + 1 + 1 + 1 = 8$

Droids are sold in boxes with 3 droids in each box.
If Luke bought 5 boxes, how many droids did he buy altogether?

$3 + 3 + 3 + 3 + 3 = 15$

Chewbacca and Han have to paint 6 rooms.
Each room needs 2 cans of paint. How many cans of paint do they need to do all 6 rooms?

$2 + 2 + 2 + 2 + 2 + 2 = 12$

Each dewback needs to drink 2 buckets of water every day. How many buckets of water are needed for 4 dewbacks every day?

$2 + 2 + 2 + 2 = 8$

Aayla Secura can defeat 3 clone troopers every minute.
How many clone troopers can she defeat in 6 minutes?

$3 + 3 + 3 + 3 + 3 + 3 = 18$

Answers

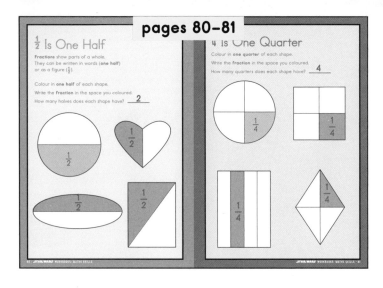

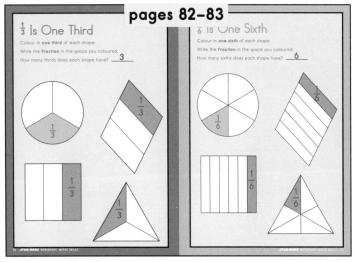

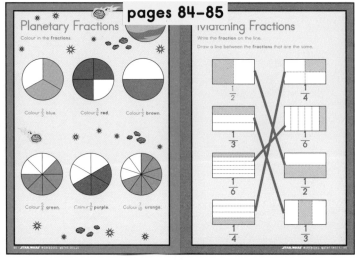

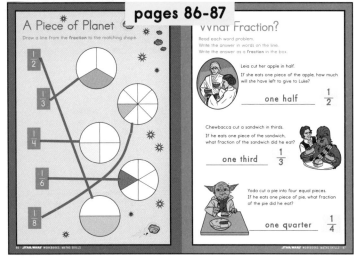

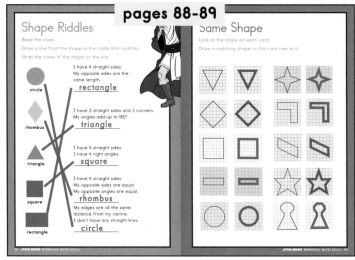

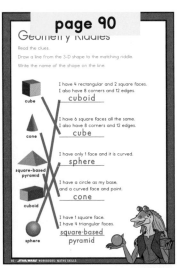